The
Power
Positive
Connections

Inspirational Stories to Lift Your Soul

Liz Hoskin

PQ Books

Published in 2022 by PQ Books

Copyright © Liz Hoskin 2022

Liz Hoskin has asserted her right to be identified as the author
of this Work in accordance with the Copyright, Designs
and Patents Act 1988

ISBN Paperback: 978-1-7396301-0-2
Ebook: 978-1-7396301-1-9

A CIP catalogue copy of this book can be
found in the British Library.

Published with the help of Indie Authors World
www.indieauthorsworld.com

IndieAuthors
World

To my husband who always believed one day I would
have a book published.

and my children who cheered me on throughout
the whole process.

A book that connects with the reader instantly. It is written from the heart and reaches your heart. Practical and inspiring, great book for those who want to connect to others with ease. The power of positive connection in practice, with truly inspiring stories.

Lydia Ann Mitchell Ph. D.
Author of *Messages from the Angel Nebula*

Want to find it easier to connect with people and make the most of life? Every moment you're with others has the potential to enrich your life and bring joy or comfort to others. That's what this book will help you do. Liz's wisdom, positivity, and desire to help others shines through the uplifting stories and practical tips she shares in this book – so you can make the most of every connection with more confidence, ease, and impact. It's time to stop letting opportunities slip through your fingers. Read this book.

Alisoun Mackenzie
Author of *Heartatude*

Liz radiates positive energy, and her personality shines through in this inspiring book. She encourages genuine, heartfelt connections and actions that really do make a difference. Great read for new and seasoned networkers, and Liz's examples show that these opportunities are all around us.

Anna Bell
Author of *Roots for Growth*

Acknowledgements

Thanks to my friend Kate for managing to get all the stories out of my head and on to paper in a week.

I would like to thank my husband, my children and friends.

To all the team at Indie Authors World for supporting me every step of the way even when I was finding it tough to get to the finishing line.

To all the amazing Connections from my stories, who contributed to my life and helped form the stories in The Power of Positive Connections.

The most important acknowledgement goes to you, our reader and remember to stay open to having a go at The Power of Positive Connections and making your very own Positive Connections along the way.

Introduction

What do you do when you are bullied so much that you end up being unable to speak, suffering from clinical depression, and experiencing burnout? You spend long times sitting about, not being able to do anything, unable to feel anything, and so numb that nothing reaches you.

This was where my journey to publishing this book began.

I was told that I wouldn't be able to work again and would probably live a very uneventful life. However, my daughter had other ideas and concocted a plan to get me out of the house and buy a book to read, as she knew that was something I had loved to do before all of this had happened.

At the outset, I'm not sure if she had an actual plan or what her expectations for me were, but she was absolutely determined to find her mum again and was sure that reading would prove to be the key.

I admit, her plan wasn't an overnight success. But one day, as I was reading the book *Succeed for Yourself* by Richard Denny, I came across a paragraph which asked what you would do if you were stuck at a red traffic light in your cabriolet with the roof down and some young boys came along and dumped their empty takeaway rubbish in your car. At that moment, I shouted out that I would be really angry and chuck it back at them. And suddenly I realised that this reflected exactly my current situation, because I had believed the 'rubbish' someone had been putting into my head (my cabriolet) and not choosing to dismiss it (or chuck it out) because it was not true. I had been too open to taking on board someone's opinion of me. That's when it dawned on me that all I had to do was shut those words out.

That was my lightbulb moment, and everything suddenly made sense! With that realisation, I was back and determined to change the world – starting with myself first.

I went back to work with my confidence and power back, and within one hour I had been made redundant and sent home on garden leave for three months. The tables had turned, because now they knew I would not put up with their behaviour any more. I was well and truly back, and it felt so good. I stood in my power and said what I was going to do, and I made sure everyone knew what had happened to me so that there was no more rubbish being said.

During that three months on garden leave, I had time to think about what I wanted to do that would fire me up every single day. That's when the idea came to me to start my own company, which I called Positive Qualities. I wanted it to be about creating positive change in businesses and people, so that they could enjoy their work. And I was determined that I was going to make a difference in so many people's lives.

My quest was started, and I was on fire. I began by reading lots of books and attending a host of courses, seminars, and conferences on positivity, the Law of Attraction, and the subconscious mind, and I consumed as much information as I could. My appetite was insatiable.

I realised that it doesn't matter what happens to you; it's how you deal with what happens to you that matters. So I began designing programmes for people to share everything I had learned, so that they too could benefit from a positive mindset leading to a positive life.

From then on, I found myself travelling all over Europe to work with some amazing companies and people, and easily making positive connections with everyone I met.

And that is where the idea for this book came from. I could see that I was onto something, as doors opened with ease, possibilities were put in front of me, and my life – both business and personally – started to fly.

You too can benefit from the Power of Positive Connection, as it follows a pattern. And once you've read this book you can sign up for my Power of Positive Connections Webinar once it's released , where I will give you the secret formula that will enable you to benefit from this amazing way to live your life.

Who knows what might happen? We might even become positive connections! However, there is one thing I'm certain of, and that is that your life will take a turn for the better.

So, read on, start looking forward to those changes – and please remember to let me know what positive connections you make!

And so It Began...

When did I start connecting positively with people? Well... during the course of my work, I attended lots of networking events and always came home feeling really dissatisfied that so many of the people I met were interested only in themselves and what they could get from me, rather than relating to me as a person. After this happened at about 20 events, I decided to do something really different. I wasn't sure what, but I was ready to try anything. You know that feeling you get in your stomach when something really exciting is going to happen? Well, I started to feel that, so I put my faith in my intuition to do what felt right, which I would then evaluate to see if it worked. There was a business event coming up for women, and I just knew that would be the time to try my new way of positively connecting with people rather than networking.

However, I had no ticket to the event and time was running out, so I phoned the ticket hotline and was told that all the tickets had been sold. This is when the words started to come out of my mouth, words that seconds earlier had not even crossed my mind, and I said to the woman on the other end of the phone, "You mean to say that if I turn up on the night, you'll turn me away?" And she replied, "Oh, I don't know about that, but there aren't any tickets left."

I said, "What about if I turn up anyway, and maybe someone will cancel and not show, so I can have their place? What do you think?"

At that moment I could sense that the woman was on my side, rooting for me. She said, "Look, turn up and I'm sure you'll get in, as you sound so excited about the event. They wouldn't dare turn you away. Good luck, and have a great time!"

I thanked her for her encouragement and came off the phone knowing I was doing the right thing. The words of the song *Ain't no Stoppin' Me Now* came into my head, and I felt I was on a mission to succeed, but in a warm and friendly way. And this felt so good that I was convinced I was finally on the right track. I phoned my friend Avril and told her what had happened, and she said she had already organised a ticket for herself so we should go together. Great idea. And the wheels were off and running.

That Friday came around so quickly, and all day I was full of excitement. I just knew everything was going to go well and we would have a fantastic time. Now it's amazing when you feel like this, because that's when great things start happening! My hair went right first time; my make-up just glided on; and I looked in the mirror and I looked so good! At that exact moment, I felt as though I could do anything, so I savoured the picture and connected the feeling it gave me, and was determined that this is what would keep me going that evening.

The train was early. It was a lovely evening, as the Edinburgh Festival was on and there was a magical party atmosphere on the train. I ended up chatting to three women who were going to the festival for the first time and, before we knew it, we were sharing our life stories and making each other laugh, so the journey passed in a flash. As we arrived at Waverley Station, we wished each other well, gave each other a hug, then went our separate ways. (They were very similar ways. However, at that time, I didn't know this.) My friend Avril appeared, and when I got into her car, I told her about my journey and we both laughed and thought how great things happen when you least expect them. Now I know differently…

When we arrived at the event, I spoke to the woman on the registration desk, who was extremely nice and friendly. "Of course, you can come in!" she told me. "Here's a badge." She then checked my name off, as it turned out that the lovely lady I had spoken to on the telephone had added me to the list after all.

Connection No. 1
Catherine

First Impressions and Intuition

This story is about not judging people on first impressions, as you will miss out on some fantastic positive connections if you do.

By not judging you will meet people from all different backgrounds: some will become lifelong friends; some will share a common bond; others will be happy to have met you just for a short while.

Also, it is important to listen to your intuition. If you ignore it, you may miss out on an opportunity to find the answer you've been searching for!

Wow! Something magical was happening. As we walked upstairs to the event, I couldn't help but feel excitement. I still had no idea what was about to happen, however I just knew it was going to be good.

Everything kicked into action when we went to the buffet. I felt like a Belisha Beacon as I started to attract people in the queue. It was as if I had a magnet, and everyone was being pulled towards me. That's when it struck me that this was happening because I was giving off loads of positive energy, and I was attracting people who wanted to share my energy. We all enjoyed quick, happy connections, and everyone I spoke to was full of anticipation for the night ahead.

Let me describe the room for you. There were lots of women in sombre business suits with sombre faces; not at all friendly. Also, there were women who were very colourful and looked like they would burst if they couldn't talk to someone. These colourful women looked more positive than the 'suits' who were all stuck together. I had expected this to be a networking event where people came to meet new people, but these 'suits' didn't look too friendly or open to meeting anyone. I decided it was time for some improvisation to make them join in.

I picked out one woman who looked interesting. She had red highlights in her hair, and she was my first 'experiment'. I went over to her and introduced myself and I said, "Hi, my name is Liz Hoskin. My company is called Positive Qualities. We all have lots of Positive Qualities. However, we lose them from time to time and I help you get them back."

She introduced herself as Catherine who ran a company specialising in Customer Service Training.

"Me too!" I squealed in delight. "I do Customer Service Training using positive language."

I could see her starting to warm to me, and she began to tell me a bit about her hopes and aspirations. I explained that my long-term goal was to be a motivational speaker and to take the Scottish style of motivation to America.

She then said, "You should be the speaker tonight, as the one who is scheduled tells the same story all the time, and it would be nice to hear something new."

I replied, "Yes, it would be great, but there's always new information we can pick up, and we don't always listen as effectively as we think we do."

She laughed in agreement, and that was the beginning. We sat down together, and Catherine introduced me to her colleagues sitting beside her.

She was right about the speaker! I had heard the story before. Never mind, though; the night was still young, and the networking was still to come. At that moment, the speaker finished, and they announced that networking was about to begin. We were all to make sure to leave our details with the girl at the desk because there was a Prize Draw for £100 worth of business books. At a quick glance, I could see they were my favourite books. This had been a fun night so far, and to win the books would make it even better.

At that, my friend Avril said, "I never win anything, and I would really like to win these books."

I replied, "Stop being so negative. If you focus on being more positive, you might just win them." I asked her, "Why do you want these books, Avril?"

She said she wanted the one on marketing as she believed it would help increase her business. So I told her, "Go and register your details, and tell the girl that you're looking forward to her call when you win!"

We both laughed as we both went to register. This perked Avril up a bit, and she really went for it. (I will tell you later what happened.)

No-one was networking. They were all just standing around the room, avoiding eye contact or standing with the people they had come along with. That's when it struck me that no-one had given directions on how to network, and everyone was waiting for someone else to make the first move. Being an Activist/Pragmatist – more importantly, an Activist/Pragmatist on a mission! – I felt it was my responsibility to make things happen.

I looked around and spotted four women holding onto the wall, trying to look invisible and seeming really nervous. I walked up to them and said, "Nights like these are very nerve-wracking, especially when you don't know anyone here."

They all chipped in, almost in unison, that this was the scariest thing they had ever done. Once I got them talking, I asked what they each did for a living. One had come along to support her friend who wanted to be an aromatherapist, but didn't know how to go about it.

And then the magic happened again when I said, "You'll never believe it! I have a good friend who runs a very successful aromatherapy business. Would you like me to get her to phone you and you could ask her how she got started?"

The woman almost fainted. She couldn't believe her luck. She then started talking very excitedly about she had nearly backed out of the evening, but something had made her come. Now she knew what! The magic?

The other woman was training to be a book-keeper, and I told her, "You've guessed it already, but I have a really good friend who's an accountant and she will be happy to point you in the right direction."

We all swapped details, and I left four very happy, animated women who would already rate this as a brilliant event, as something truly magical had happened to them.

On a roll, I started moving around the room, but the next bit was bolder as I started matching people up. I found more bookkeepers, accountants, customer service people, aromatherapists and, before I knew it, there was a small crowd forming around me, all wanting help or just to share in the buzz of the moment.

Then one woman came up to me and said, "I need your help. My boyfriend and I are moving to Barcelona and are starting a juice business, and we're not sure where we'll get funding." What a challenge! But within five minutes I had helped her with an outline of where she might source funding for her project. The ideas came into my mind in a flash, and I was really onto something.

Before I knew it, the event had come to an end, but what an evening!

You might be asking yourself what I got out of that evening. Well, for me, the joy on those women's faces was enough. I left with a feeling of true accomplishment and an understanding that anyone can make a difference in other people's lives. All you have to do is make an effort.

The next morning, I got a phone call from my friend Avril. And yes, you've guessed it – she had won the books. She was absolutely ecstatic, walking on air.

I was thrilled for her, and over the moon at what I had achieved at the event. It was a feeling I excitedly wanted to repeat. But when?

Connection No. 2
Eva

Make the Most of Every Opportunity

This story holds a special place in my heart, as it happened at a time of great change in my business when I was being pulled in many different directions. The principles of the Power of Positive Connection never leave you, as long as you believe in helping others and making the most of each and every opportunity.

In one positive connection there is usually more than one opportunity – try it and find out for yourself.

You know when you're onto a Positive Connection as that's when coincidences start jumping out in front of you to prove to you that you're on the right track!

Not long after the business event, I was asked to attend the Scottish Women's Awards, which celebrates and recognises Scottish female talent. As it was a very posh function in Edinburgh, everyone was dressed up to the nines. Unusually for me, though, I was feeling slightly apprehensive that night due to the sheer numbers in attendance.

We were all ushered through to the pre-dinner drinks where everyone (again) was just standing around, not interacting. It looked like they were sizing up the competition and looking at each other's outfits. That's when I noticed a woman with the most fantastic diamond earrings which made her sparkle. I decided to go across to speak to her because I wanted to know where she got them. She was absolutely delighted that someone loved her earrings, and she immediately took them off and asked if I wanted to try them on. I said, "No, no, no. They look fantastic on you. As long as I know the shop where you bought them, that will do me for tonight." And then it started again…

We began chatting about the usual stuff – what we did for a living, our hopes and aspirations, etc – and before we knew it, we had an audience and lots of women wanted to join in the conversation. It was absolutely fantastic how the atmosphere had suddenly changed from being cold and unfriendly to being warm and inclusive.

At that point, we were requested to take our seats at our tables. There was a real buzz in the room as we found our seats. We discovered we were at adjacent tables, so we were able to carry on chatting as before.

*

Eva was the waitress on our table for the evening. She was obviously aware of the First Five Minutes – that's the time it takes to either click or decide to move on (a more in-depth explanation is near the end of this book). Her customer care was excellent and she couldn't do enough for us. When she asked me if I wanted more wine, I heard her accent and asked where she came from. She said she was from Spain.

I said, "Surely this isn't what you do for a living?"

She replied, "Ah no, I just do this to help with my studies. I'm in my final year of Business Studies in Edinburgh."

"Do you have a job lined up for when you finish your course?" I asked.

"No, I've been finding it very difficult," she admitted, "and I think I might have to go back to Spain."

When I asked her if that's what she wanted, she told me, "No. I love Scotland."

And then it started again… and you're never going to believe this!

I told her, "At the moment, I'm working on a project which involves a Spanish bank in Glasgow."

She was amazed that there was such a thing in Scotland, as she hadn't realised. Then I told her that I would pass her details on to the Manager of that bank, and although I couldn't make any promises, we had nothing to lose by giving it a go. She wrote her details on the back of one of my business cards and continued her evening with an even bigger smile.

My dinner companions wanted to know what had just taken place, and I explained that this is the sort of thing I do for people – putting them in touch with others; in other words, connecting people. At first, there were a few negative comments, with some saying that it was dangerous to go about promising things to people. However, I pointed out that I had made no promises. If something came of it, good and well, and I knew that Eva fully appreciated that. My explanation seemed to satisfy them for the moment, and we had a wonderful evening.

So, do you want to hear what happened next?

The following Monday morning I went to see the Manager of the Spanish bank and told him about Eva. He said, "Funny you should tell me that. I have a couple of people from Edinburgh already working here, and she might manage to get a lift with them if things work out!"

I left him in good faith that things would happen. And three weeks later, I received an email, which said: "*Thank you so much. I have been offered a job, and I am so happy! Sunshine & smiles, Eva.*"

Connection No 3
Brian

The Answer is Right in Front of You

This story is about one of my many positive connections whilst flying – which is a great way to try out the principles, as you have a captive audience. And before you ask: No, I have never been asked/told to shut up or shove off!

I believe that this is because of the principles and my belief in them, plus I have been practising for a while now, and even if I say it myself, I'm pretty good at the Power of Positive Connection!

Sometimes in life the answer is right in front of you, however you just need someone to help you work that out!

Brian is a property developer I met on a flight coming back from Heathrow to Edinburgh. We were sitting on the plane when the announcement was made that the flight had been delayed. As sometimes happens, we looked at each other and said at exactly the same time, "Looks like we're really going to be here for some time." That made us both laugh. And it happened again…

I asked him what he did for a living, and he told me. Then he asked what I did, and at that time I was doing training. He replied, and I kid you not, "Do you do this often?"

I laughed at his comment and said, "Ah, the old ones are the best!"

Our conversation then turned to families. He had two boys and a girl, and I have a boy and a girl. I told him my two were off school the following week for half-term, and he asked what school they went to.

When I told him Dollar Academy, he said, "Funny you should say that! My wife and I have been busy looking for a school in the Edinburgh area, as we're not happy with their current school."

I told him they had been looking in the wrong place, and went on to explain the unique motivational ethos at Dollar Academy and suggested he contact the Rector. The annual entrance exam had passed, but I assured him that as Dollar was a business, I felt there was a chance they could sort something out. We discussed what the entrance exam involved, and I explained that I had coached my kids through the test and was happy to let him borrow my books. We swapped email addresses and I promised to send him the information on Dollar Academy as soon as I reached home.

As we were getting on so well, he gave me another opening because he had a problem with his car. The garage concerned was refusing to give him the service history of his car, and because I had previously worked in the motor industry, I was able to tell him his rights and how to go about getting his desired outcome.

He said, "This has been an absolutely fantastic journey. The best value for money I've ever had on a flight. I sat beside a complete stranger, and I've now sorted out a couple of things that were on my mind!".

When I reached home that night, I sent him an email with all the relevant details about my children's school and also wished him luck with his car.

The following day (not three weeks this time!), I received an email from Brian thanking me for the information and taking me up on my offer to borrow my coaching books for his children. I replied immediately to say that I was going to his local station the following evening so could drop the books off at his house, if that was OK. He emailed straight back to say it was, and that's exactly what I did.

Some weeks later, I received another email telling me that his children were sitting their entrance exam that week and hoped everything would go well. A couple of weeks later, another email from Brian: "Passed. Thanks a million! Kids start at new term!"

Wow, I was really getting the hang of this. But there's more…

Once the new term was underway, my daughter Cara came home from school one day and asked me what the children of the man in the plane were called. I told her and she said: "Mum, they get on my bus, and they're really nice." I reminded Cara to tell the children that the woman on the plane was really pleased that they had been accepted into Dollar Academy. A few nights later, Cara came home with my coaching books.

It gets better. They asked to borrow the books again for their next child, and this time Cara was the postwoman. The good news is that their child was accepted as well, so all three of his children are at the same school.

It gets even better. When we went to Parents' Night at the school, Brian and his wife came up to thank me and I introduced them to my husband, David. Brian told him he had an amazing wife and added, "Is there anything she can't fix?"

My husband replied, "Haven't found it yet."

Footnote: Brian got his car sorted to his great satisfaction, by doing what I suggested.

Connection No. 4
Stephen

The First Five Minutes

This story could have got off to a wrong start if I hadn't followed the principle about First Impressions in Connection One. Wow. this stuff really works! I believe that the first five minutes of any connection are vital to its outcome. Because if you don't establish rapport or get the situation you find yourself in off to a positive start in the first five minutes, it may be extremely difficult to make a positive connection. Stephen was very angry with the world in general, and if I had been put off by this, I would never have shared the First Five Minutes with him and let him do something for himself for once.

Stephen was a challenge. I had the doubtful privilege of being driven to London's Heathrow Airport in his taxi. What a ride that was! From the moment I met him, all he could do was to vent his spleen at the world. He didn't have a good word to say about anything or anyone. So, when he asked me which terminal I wanted, I couldn't even remember because it had been such a stressful journey. Then he started again…

I felt I had to get through to Stephen in some way, so every time he took a breath, I asked a question, which helped me put names to the people he was talking about. Before long, I had his life story. He was not a happy chappie.

When we arrived at the terminal, I felt compelled to share with him something from my training days which I felt would turn his life around if he cared enough to put it into practice. It's what I call "The First Five Minutes". He was intrigued enough to listen to my passion, and I then spelt out what I meant.

There are three times in most people's day when it's particularly important to make an effort which sets the tone for the rest day:

> First thing in the morning, it's really important to get out of the right side of the bed. Know what I mean? The first five minutes of your day, upon opening your eyes, telling yourself what kind of day you're going to have will affect your mood for the rest of that day.

> The second time is when you arrive at work. The first five minutes are crucial as you interact with your colleagues. What

you say and do affects others, and you. If you take time to smile, show an interest in them, ask them how their evening went, etc – it all makes a difference. That then impacts the rest of your day and theirs, including how you answer the phone, your conduct at meetings, and so on.

> And the third, and perhaps most important, time is when you arrive home in the evening. Take time to greet your partner, children, or pet (whatever you've got), and ask them about their day before launching into your story. This will set the tone for evening and help you relax, recover, and rejuvenate, ready for another day.

Coincidentally, three weeks later (again!), I happened to be down in London on business again. I needed to get to Heathrow, and who should meet and greet me but Stephen. No, let's correct that, the new Stephen. What a transformation. He opened my door, made sure I was comfortable, and asked how my day was. It was poetry in motion, just wonderful. He then related the impact my advice had had on his and his family's life. And boy, what a story!

It's such a simple thing, but you never know what will happen when you do this.

Connection No. 5
Chris and Multiple Connections

Follow Your Dreams

This story will inspire you to experiment with the Power of Positive Connection, as this all happened to me in the space of three weeks, and boy did I follow my dreams!

All the situations in this story happened as the result of me attending a self-development seminar in London Arena, and listening to my intuition and going with the moment. This took great courage, as I was dealing with connections from all over the world and travelling to different countries as a result.

A few years ago – this time in Glasgow – I met a lady called Chris, who asked me what I really did for a living because she didn't believe that I was a Project Manager in a bank, which is where we met. I felt it was so right to share with her what I really do. When I told her that I was a motivational speaker and trainer, she said, "I knew it, I just knew it!"

She told me I was far too bubbly and vibrant to be doing a boring bank job. I then gave her my business card, brochure, and bookmark and she loved the colours I had used. We then went on to the "Me Too's" – books we'd read, goals we'd set, seminars we'd attended – and then she asked if I knew anything about Anthony Robbins.

And that opened up a whole new chapter…

I knew about Tony Robbins from my days of being a Financial Consultant. Also, I had seen a couple of his videos, one of which was on goal-setting. At that time, he hadn't set the heather on fire for me.

However, Chris told me, "You need to see him live, and I know where you can get a ticket at a reasonable price for his next seminar in London in three weeks' time." That magical number three again! (The number three is linked to harmony and optimism.)

My Scottishness kicked in and I asked her, "What is a reasonable price to a Scotswoman, come on?"

She laughed and said she would get a ticket for me at a discount price.

Then I asked her, "What about accommodation, and flights? How am I going to do all this?"

She replied, "Go home and think about it over the weekend, and I will let you know on Monday."

I did. I went home and discussed it with my husband, and next thing I knew I was on a plane to London, with accommodation taken care of by Chris, who very kindly arranged for me to stay at her friend's flat.

What an experience!

On arrival, I was told to look out for Kate – another one of Chris's friends who was crewing at the seminar and would look after me. And you'll never believe it. Who was the first person I met when I went through the doors?

Once registered, I went for a bite to eat and found a café round the corner with an empty table so that I could do a bit of people-watching. I had just taken a bite from a sandwich when a couple asked if they could join me, and naturally I agreed. And that's how I met Rema and Evan.

We exchanged pleasantries to get the conversation going, and lo and behold they were attending the same seminar, which was called "Unleash the Power Within". At the time, I wasn't sure what was wrong with Evan, but I knew he wasn't well as he had a dull complexion, and his energy was heavy. Once we got to know each other a little more, Evan told me that for the last 23 years he had been dying with cancer.

My training in positive language came to the fore and I replied, "Evan, you've got it round the wrong way. You've been living with cancer for 23 years."

This was a revelation and an emotional experience for him, but I pointed out, "If you've managed to live for 23 years with cancer, let's see how many more years you can go."

It was such a fantastic experience for all of us, because Rema had accompanied Evan to the seminar simply to support him, but now he felt able to do it for himself which freed her up to enjoy the event. And she cried because she had seen the change in Evan at first hand and was relieved and excited for him all at once.

Once inside the London Arena we took our places in the second row from the front and the music, dancing, and atmosphere kicked in. When the BIG MAN appeared to get the show on the road, he asked us all to turn to our left and introduce ourselves, and that's how I met James.

He said, "Hi, I'm James, and I come from Polmont."

I replied, "My name is Liz and I come from Stenhousemuir, and I want a refund! I've come all this way, and in a crowd of 5,000 people I meet someone from four miles down the road."

I had known that I was there for a reason, and maybe the fact he was local to me, I wondered if he might have been that reason. Then we began our connection…

We had a lot in common (what I call Me Too's), and I knew this was going to be an event to remember.

On the third day – after having had very little to eat – we were absolutely starving and decided to take ourselves off to the nearest Chinese restaurant at the first interval. In the previous two days of the seminar, during one of the exercises I had set myself some short-terms goals, such as "Work in Ireland; Increase my fees; Go to America; and Drive in a Limo".

When we arrived at the Chinese restaurant, there was a wedding reception so we had to queue for an interminable half hour, and my stomach thought my throat had been cut. Then it started again…

The woman in front of me in the queue had obviously heard my accent, and she turned round and asked, "Oh, you're from Scotland. What part do you come from?"

I said, "I come from Stenhousemuir, which has a football team which is usually known as 'Stenhousemuir Nil'." That caused a laugh, then I added, "We also have the most fantastic toffee factory."

It turned out that the woman, who was Irish, had heard about the company and said it was her favourite toffee. Then she asked me, "So, what do you do for a living?"

Magical words came out of my mouth, which I don't normally say. I replied, "I'm a Call Centre Doctor, because I fix sick call centres." At that time I was working on a Call Centre Project for the bank, and the call centre was needing a lot of love and attention.

She said, "You're never going to believe this, but we've got a sick call centre!" Then she turned round and introduced me to her husband, who invited me to have dinner with them… which let me jump the queue, much to other people's disgust.

The upshot of this experience, though, was that I didn't get to enjoy my Chinese meal because they asked so many questions. Our time ran out, and we had to return to the seminar.

Before leaving the restaurant, we exchanged details, and her husband said he would give me a call the following day to arrange for me to visit their sick call centre in Ireland.

So, what happened next? Well, he didn't call me, so I went home feeling slightly disappointed.

However, the day after that, he did call and asked, "Have you ever been to Ireland?"

I said I hadn't, but that it was one of my new goals from the seminar. Long story short, I went to work in Ireland the following week for two days. (By the way, I also increased my fees before committing to the work.)

And it happened again…

On the second day, he asked me to stay a third day because he wanted me to meet people and to get a better idea of everything that needed to be done. On the third day, he asked me if I had ever been to America. The way my life was going at that time, I anticipated what he was going to say next, which was: "Would you like to go to America?"

He had booked a conference there but was unable to attend, so he wanted me to go on his behalf. He said he would call me that Saturday to make final arrangements, and this time he did call as promised. By the Sunday night, I was in Chicago.

Arriving at Chicago's O'Hare Airport, I decided to fulfil my third goal, which was to ride in a limo. I was on a roll, and I duly did it, causing some excitement at the hotel. When I arrived, I had six porters wanting to assist with my one suitcase, which we all had a good laugh about. I had never before been able to achieve goals so quickly and with so little effort. The difference was the positive connections I was making with so many people I met, which seemed to flow and add momentum to my clear goals.

Try it for yourself. Genuinely connect with people. What you give out, you get back in abundance.

At the International Call Centre Management Conference in Chicago (I kid you not), I ended up on the front page of the conference magazine by connecting with one of their reporters, with whom I shared a story of a happy customer ending. The conference itself was stimulating because there were lots of interesting people to connect with. And did I connect? You bet!

I was attracted to a stand that offered call centre recording equipment, because all the people looked happy and one woman in particular caught my attention. Then it started again…

When talking to Maureen, I found out she was getting married in the Fall (autumn) in New York, and she was at pains to work out which hairstyle would suit her because she had shoulder-length hair and wore glasses. We discussed all the options available, then I had the most fantastic idea: she should take a digital picture then log onto one of the make-over sites on the internet, where she could check out objectively the hairstyle that would suit her best, without making the mistake of a horrible haircut which would ruin her wedding day. All women know that if your hair is right, everything else falls into place for you.

Maureen was absolutely delighted because she had not thought of that, and the issue had really been bugging her. So I promised to send her a link to the site when I returned home, which I did. I received a lovely email back from Maureen saying it had been the best thing ever, as it had opened her mind up to new hairstyles she had never even thought about. One happy bride-to-be! Who said conferences had to be all about work? Grab the opportunity to connect with people anywhere on any subject.

And it doesn't stop there. At another stand I met a Canadian lady who had been watching me watching her connecting with all different nationalities at the conference – unlike her neighbouring colleagues. It was a case of like attracting like, and she told me later that she had been wondering how long it would take me to come and speak to her. Just let's say that we shared a lot of Me Too's, had photographs taken together, and promised to work together some time in the future. See you soon I hope, Berta.

Are you beginning to get the picture about what you can do to connect? It's all about your attitude.

Connection No. 6
Leigh and Vicky

Be Prepared

This story is all about considering the possibilities available to you and how, with proper preparation, you can achieve your target as long as you keep it firmly in your sights. It's also about not being put off when you don't get the job you thought was yours, as it usually means that something even better is just around the corner.

I met Leigh when I gave a presentation at the company where she worked before being made redundant. She had worked for them since she left school and had never thought she could do anything else. At the end of my presentation, she approached me to confirm to herself that she couldn't possibly do it, but instead, I talked her through how it would be possible. I'd analysed that she was a team player, responsible for her own productivity but who understood the impact that had on her team. And as a customer services operator, that was one of the most important parts of the job. She got really excited that she could go for that type of job, and redundancy no longer terrified her.

Leigh started working with me and turned out to be one of the best customer services operators I have ever had, because she truly cared about the customers she dealt with. When I was offered another opportunity that I couldn't refuse, she shared with me one of her big goals about working in a bank. I got her to talk me through exactly what she wanted. She felt that working in a bank would give her status and security – two things which were important to her, but which she had always thought were beyond her reach because she left school with few formal qualifications. I let her borrow one of my books which prepared her mentally for her assessment and interview, then I coached her through this process so that she could personalise the answers.

As it began to dawn on her that her ultimate job was within her reach, she became really excited and realised that it was up to her to make a success of her opportunity. She told me the date of her interview and showed me the outfit she was going to wear, and we both agreed that she looked the part, i.e., professional. I wished her all the best and one month later she rang to let me know she had been successful. In fact, I was now talking to the new Customer Services Officer for that bank! What a turnaround.

But it underlines that you don't have to accept anything less. With a bit of self-belief and some encouragement, you can be just about anything you want to be.

Next time someone says, "I could never do that," ask them why they think that way, because you, too, can be their source of encouragement. It does not take training or qualifications to provide encouragement. It just takes a little effort and an interest in others. Who knows, you might impact someone's life more than you'll ever know. To encourage yourself and others more, ask people to let you know the outcome, which may begin another chapter…

…called 'Keeping it in the Family', because I got to know Leigh's sister, Vicky, who came to me because Leigh shared how I had helped her.

Vicky also wanted to work in a bank (what's the attraction?), but deep down that really was NOT what she wanted, although she didn't know it then. Again, I let her borrow my book and coached her through the process for her assessment and interview. This time, though, it was a totally different story. She didn't get the job, which was a huge surprise to her, but I wasn't the least surprised as I felt she was destined for other things.

After a huge post-mortem, it transpired that Vicky was happy working in a call centre but not the one she was in. So she applied to a couple of other call centres, and this time she was successful. Vicky loved interacting with people over the phone, and as a result of this passion she is now a trainer for the same organisation. It has proved to be quite an eye-opener for her. She's committed to her job, is now very career-minded, and is having a wonderful time into the bargain.

Connection No. 7
Lesley

Blank Sheet

This story is about using the technique of blank sheet to discover your true passion, especially when something happens in your life that forces you to look for a change. Instead of being a victim and feeling sorry for yourself, this story opens you up to the opportunities out there for you to claim as your own.

I met Lesley on a flight from Edinburgh to London Heathrow. This most gorgeous girl came onto the flight, and I wanted her to sit beside me because she looked like she had a story to tell – and you know, she did! As soon as she sat down, boy did we ever connect! It was one of the quickest connections I've every made.

She said to me, "Business or pleasure?"

I said, "Business," and asked her the same question.

She replied, "Pleasure."

I thought she was a model, so I asked her where she was going. She explained that she was going on holiday to Egypt, and it all fell into place for me. It was obvious she had a love for Egypt because of its subtle influence in her style of make-up and clothing. I admitted that it was a place I had always wanted to visit, so I was given a marvellous tour of Egypt, with her as the guide! Her descriptions and stories brought the place to life for me even more, and she was so animated as we were conversing (just my kind of person).

She explained that she had been visiting the country for a number of years and had made friends with an Egyptian family, which was what drew her back each time. Once she had told me all about Egypt, I asked what she did for a living. Surprisingly, she worked as a clerk in Edinburgh, but was suffering from RSI and was looking for a change of occupation. Then it started…

I said, "You'll never believe what I do for a living. I help people find their passion! I do this using an exercise called the 'Blank Sheet'. Are you up for having a go?"

She said, "You bet!" (Amusingly, our nearest neighbour became very interested and listened to everything we discussed!)

By using the Blank Sheet exercise, Lesley discovered she had two overriding passions in life. One was a love of criminal court cases (mine not to ask why), and the other was of course Egypt. What we decided then was to look at each one separately to find her No. 1 passion.

No, Egypt didn't win. Crime did. She wanted to write crime novels, which was a huge surprise to me… and to her! But a simple process of elimination led us on to making a plan together of how she could enter this field. Sadly, our flight ended just as we put the finishing touches to her plan.

However, she was so delighted at the unexpected turn of events on what could have been an uneventful flight that we exchanged details and. I suggested she get in touch further if there was anything else I could help with. We left as friends, with a big hug in the terminal before she went for her next connection… to Egypt.

To date, she has not been in touch, but perhaps I should get in touch with her. Sometimes you have to take the initiative. As in all the best crime novels, I would love to know what happened next.

Connection No. 8
Rhona

Make the Effort

This story is all about Making A Difference by going that little bit further, and making an effort to keep going even when you feel you have a result. It's all about raising your game and reaping the rewards that go with it.

How did I connect with Rhona? She was recommended to me by an accountant who said she was the most positive bank manager she knew and that we would both benefit from connecting. (By that time, I was facilitating motivational/networking lunches for business people in central Scotland.) Rhona duly came along to my lunches and enjoyed them enormously. One day in particular had a huge impact on her. It was the day of my M.A.D. (Making A Difference, for the uninitiated) talk, when I spoke about making a little more effort in your life, just going that little bit further, and how you never know what you might achieve.

With those words ringing in her ears, Rhona decided to make a difference in her business life. She wanted to step up to get the recognition she deserved, as she was the only female bank manager in her area. For a sportsmen's dinner taking place at the end of the month, she wanted sponsorship from local businesses for several raffle prizes, rather than just one. Before she left our lunch venue, she had already got her first sponsorship, and this set the ball rolling for what happened next. By the end of the day, she had four impressive raffle prizes and a huge sense of satisfaction.

The following day, Rhona rang to update me on the success she had had and was enthusing about how easy it had been. One particular sponsor seemed to have caught Rhona's eye and she had arranged to have lunch with him later that week. A business lunch, of course. I wasn't convinced, though, because by the way she spoke about him, I knew this was going to be a different type of connection.

A week later I heard how her lunch had progressed. She was thrilled with the Me Too's they had shared and that she felt so comfortable with him. My intuition was right, and she laughed when I said that she had made a **real positive connection** there.

But the story doesn't stop there. Rhona had found what she had been looking for but never expected to find – her next husband. They got engaged, and everything seemed to be going really well for them when Rhona found out she had cancer. They kept on seeing each other and he was her rock, helping her through her treatment and planning their future together. Her two daughters got on well with him, and he helped her sort out all her affairs so that she didn't need to worry about anything else.

They set their wedding date and were looking forward to their special day when Rhona had a relapse, and they were told that her time was limited. The wedding was brought forward, and they did get married, and I can imagine how happy they both were to have made it happen together.

Not long after Rhona was married, she became very ill, and I arranged to visit her in the hospice. Unfortunately, I was too late. But no-one needed to tell me that, because when I was making my way up the driveway, there was a huge rainbow over the hospice, and I was overcome with a sense of peace. At that moment I just knew she had gone.

Dear readers, this story is so special as it let my dear friend Rhona have a last chance at being truly happy. And she was.

Connection No. 9
Alex

Positive Action Plan

This story is about how to keep going every day, even when you don't feel like it. It's about adopting a positive approach to everything that you do and the techniques that can make this even easier for you.

Alex is the lawyer who helped with the lease for my business premises, and I was happily able to help him develop a positive action plan for his life.

He was introduced to me by one of my positive connections from the aforementioned Tony Robbins' seminar. When we met, and after I had dealt with the lease, I found myself spending time with him, talking about his life and what he wanted to achieve. It transpired that he'd been let down rather badly by a previous business partner and was struggling to keep on track. I simply reflected what he said to me to let him realise how negative he sounded, and explained that if he remained that way his life would not change. As a result of his recent experiences, he was rather cynical about my comments, and I knew that this was not going to be an easy connection to begin with.

I taught him a few techniques which I use in business to maintain my motivation, and there were a couple that resonated with him, including "The First Five Minutes" (explained earlier) and "Flip the Coin". In other words, flip the coin by turning negatives to positives. For example, instead of saying he was bogged down with paperwork, he could say, "I am really getting through all my paperwork today." Small changes, perhaps, but they would result in major shifts in his outlook.

As the weeks passed, Alex started to make changes, which I could see when our paths crossed. On one occasion he admitted that some days he found my advice easy to follow, and other days less so. Another time he asked me, "How do you keep yourself motivated every day?"

I told him about a positive action plan book that I use, and he asked me to tell him more about that. Rather than explain it, I said I would pop in the following day and talk him through it. When I arrived the next day, he was full of anticipation and excited to see me. The book in question was exactly what he was looking for, because it talks the reader through a positive action for EVERY day of the year – leaving no excuse for not thinking positively. We discussed how he was going to implement the plan and I left him feeling good about his future.

Latest update? He's doing really well, and he still has my book. (May I have it back, please, Alex?)

Oh, about my business lease. In the end, I never did move into those premises. The property was flooded, and I couldn't wait for the damage to be put right. The funny thing is that at that time I received a phone call letting me know that I could have a gallbladder operation if I was free. Clearly, those premises were not meant for me at that time.

And the reason I got my operation so quickly was as a result of another positive connection I made with the Consultant's PA. If you and I ever connect, I will be happy to tell you that story!

It's all about connections.

Connection No. 10
Damien

Ask the Obvious Question!

This story is about stopping to ask the obvious question before you go off avoiding a situation, otherwise you could find yourself on a long journey which takes you even further away from the thing you're avoiding. The next time you prevent yourself from getting in touch with someone because of your What If's, ask yourself the obvious question... and then get cracking.

Damien had worked in radio production. When he attended one of my call centre training seminars, I got a chance to chat with him over coffee and I asked him why he was working in a call centre. He said he had tried different jobs, none of which he particularly liked, so he thought he had nothing to lose by trying a call centre which was part of a growing employment market.

Because I love to know what makes people tick, I asked him to talk me through all the different jobs he had tried, and as he described them, I could see and hear that none of them had excited him. Except when he mentioned the radio company. When I asked why he left that job, which was the only time he showed real animation in his descriptions, he explained that he'd had a very difficult boss who he found impossible to work with, so he simply had to leave.

I wanted to do a reality check with him, so I asked him what was obvious to me: "Why have you not returned to radio production?"

He replied with a What If, as in, "What if my old boss is still there? I couldn't possibly go back."

Again, I asked the (to me) obvious question: "Have you bothered to find out if he's still there?"

At this, he seemed to go into deep, silent contemplation. Then the penny dropped when he said, "What if I've been working in all these boring jobs for the last two years – maybe all for nothing?"

Prompting him, I asked, "What are you going to do about it then?"

He gave a wry, cheeky smile, and replied, "I suppose it's about time I found out and asked the obvious question."

He thanked me very much for listening and helping him decide what he WAS going to do next. In all, our conversation had only lasted ten minutes.

Two weeks later, when I was next delivering training in the same call centre, Damien came hurrying towards me.

"You're never going to believe this," he said. "He's long gone and I'm now back working in radio at the weekends." He explained that all his former colleagues had been really pleased to see him and wondered why he hadn't been in touch for so long. Why indeed? He told them the story about our connection and the reason why he had come back to the radio station, as he had been so stuck and needed to find something out for himself.

The next time you prevent yourself from getting in touch with someone because of your What Ifs, ask yourself the obvious question... and then get cracking.

Connection No. 11
Barbara

A Change of Direction

This story is all about helping someone by recommending a book, a website, or a connection, which will benefit them. It's also about exploring what they want to do and giving them some encouragement. Remember the healing power of doing something good for someone else can help YOU feel even better too.

I met Barbara at the airport in Dublin, Ireland, one Friday night when we were both returning to Edinburgh and our flight had been delayed. She was on her way back from a conference. I was reading a book about how to fulfil your dreams and could sense that Barbara kept looking at my book. After a couple of minutes, I flashed the cover at her and asked if she wanted to have a look. She laughed and said, "I could be doing with that book." And then it started...

I asked Barbara, "So why is a book like this important to you?"

She told me her life story, and how she had left Scotland to live in Canada where she and her husband had a farm. The farm was no longer viable, and Barbara was looking for a change of direction.

I told her, "You're never going to believe this, but I help people find their direction through my work."

She said this must be her lucky night and she was glad I had sat beside her. Through a process of elimination, using my Blank Sheet Exercise, we worked out Barbara's passion. She wanted to work in Human Relations, as she said she had worked with sheep and cows and got them to do what she wanted, so she felt she could use those skills with people!

At this we had a great laugh and agreed, "Why not? What the heck!"

I then asked what she had done so far, if anything. She admitted that she had looked at some courses, but as she hadn't been completely clear about her next move, she hadn't pursued anything yet.

To make sure she was on the right track and to give her reassurance, I recommended a book and website where she could test her perceived strengths before proceeding. She couldn't believe that in such a short space of time she had an outcome.

This time I went a stage further and gave her a referral to one of my contacts from Canada that I had met at the

Chicago conference. I suggested they get in touch, as Berta would point her in the right direction about local jobs and, even better, would be a positive connection for her as well. When I suggested that, Barbara was emotionally overwhelmed. We both knew it was so right for her.

Our flight was called, and couldn't you guess? Barbara was sitting directly behind me, so we continued our connection all the way home.

I already had my outcome, because Barbara found her change of direction and the rest was up to her.

Can *you* help someone on their way by recommending a book, website, or a connection/contact?

Connection No. 12
Aileen

Serendipity

This story is about being in the right place at the right time and open to benefit from what comes your way. You are what you think about, and this story shows you that with the right thoughts you can quickly achieve what you've set your heart on.

I met another farmer's wife when I had a motivational speaker slot at a seminar in Fife, on the east coast of Scotland. It was one of my best performance nights – you know, one of those nights where everything just goes to plan... and I have the video to prove it!

When I separated my audience into breakout groups, I had the pleasure of meeting Aileen, who wanted to know what you called it when you find the right thing at the right time.

I said, "Why, serendipity, of course. Especially when you meet Liz Hoskin!"

She asked what I meant, and I replied, "You know that moment when everything falls into place, and you know it's so right when magical things start happening?" She laughed and nodded, saying, "That's been happening to me."

I told her I had been drawn to her that night because she just looked so happy, and she explained that the reason for her happiness was because she had decided she was going to run with her business idea as a result of my talk. I encouraged her to keep with that thought and told her that this was just the beginning. I then went back to the podium, as I still had a gift of a two-hour personal coaching session to raffle. And guess who won it? How could she not? She squealed with delight, such was her pleasure, and we scheduled a date to meet up.

Two weeks later, Aileen came to my office, as arranged, for her coaching session. First off, I wanted her to decide on three outcomes from our session together and how she was going to achieve those. They were: 1) How to be able to turn around resistance from existing buyers for her healthcare products; 2) How to market her products more effectively; and 3) How to get a couple of good salespeople for her business.

The first two were really easy to deal with. When we talked them through, the way ahead was obvious to her.

The last one, however, took more time, as we had to analyse the people she had in mind, to make sure she would make the right choices. At the end of the session, Aileen left feeling full of confidence and knew what she had to do.

I received a lovely thank-you email the following day, giving me a quick update because she had acted on all three outcomes and said she would recommend me to anyone who wanted to sort their business out.

What happened next? At the next monthly seminar, she volunteered to market my services! She asked for a ten-minute slot to share her experience and the results.

Serendipity in motion.

What are your outcomes? How will you connect and help others to achieve their outcomes?

Connection No. 13
Nigel

Positive Momentum

This story highlights how you can have a lot in common with the person you meet and get on so easily that when it's time to leave them, you want to do a bit more for them. It lets you see that if it is a true positive connection, you will be compelled to give them something to help them maintain momentum.

I met Nigel in Dublin, Ireland, during another of my training trips. Our initial connection was founded on Me Too's, as regards the most effective ways to do tele-marketing. As this is one of my strengths, I was able to quickly point out the pros and cons of tele-marketing. This led on to a discussion about his job, how dissatisfied he was, and that he felt the need for a change. The one thing he felt that was stopping him was that he found it very hard to remain positive. His words.

Of course, I jumped in with reassurance and tips before we headed off in different directions, although I knew that we might possibly meet up later in that same hotel. As we parted, I was convinced that Nigel needed something more.

Once my training was finished that day, I headed for the shops to buy some family presents. As my family all love books, the first place I visited was a bookstore. In front of me was a book containing positive affirmations for every day of the year. Just the thing for Nigel! I bought it, had it wrapped, and the following day it was accepted by a very grateful Nigel. It was *exactly* what he was looking for.

Many months later, when I was back in Dublin, I met Nigel again, and the first thing he said was, "That book is brilliant. It's really keeping me on track. You were so kind."

A case of a positive connection leading to maintaining positive momentum.

Do you need some positive momentum in your life?

Connection No. 14
Amy

What's Your Passion?

This story is about rallying to someone's assistance and not thinking about the consequences. This usually leads to another interesting thing about the Power of Positive Connection; it's the Universe's way of connecting you to someone whom you can help even more than you first thought.

At another businesswomen's dinner in Edinburgh, I met Amy. Again, she was a waitress at that time, and she dropped her plates at my table. You may ask, what's interesting about broken crockery? Not a thing, but it led to a connection.

Helping Amy to regain composure, we got talking and I asked her (that question again!) what she really did for a living. She said she had just qualified as a marine biologist and wanted to work with dolphins.

I laughed and said, "You're never going to believe this, but this morning on a flight down to London, I read an article in the airline's magazine about a new marine complex in Dubai, which included details about a project on dolphins."

Her face lit up because, for months, this was the answer she had been searching for. I suggested she get in touch with the airline's magazine or go online and search for the magazine. She thanked me very much, as this had opened up her mind to other areas of research. For the rest of the evening, she was more than helpful and so excited about what lay ahead.

Why did I read that article that morning?

Connection No. 15
Ahmed

Step-by-Step

This story is all about when the tables get turned on you and someone asks *you* lots of questions, as they instantly see the value of what you have. It's a nice way to connect, and it certainly keeps you on your toes. The Positive Energy flows thick and fast, and it's as though you are both on fire as you share ideas and information. When this happens, you were both definitely meant to meet, because the teacher shows up when the student is ready.

Ahmed is another taxi driver. He collected me from the airport in Southampton, England, and turned the tables on me by asking first, "So, what do you do?"

What a question!

Once he knew what I did for a living, Ahmed wanted to make the most of our positive connection and he was really quick on the uptake. By way of illustration, I started by explaining the First Five Minutes, and he immediately began asking questions on how he could put it into practice the very next day. No-one had ever given him such pointers before, and he wasn't going to let me go without fully understanding whatever it was we talked about.

We finished that first conversation just as we reached my hotel, whereupon he said, "I need to find out more information from you."

My reply was, "If it's meant to be, it will be." I told him where I would be working next day and that I would need to leave my hotel around 8am. He said, "Right, you're on. I'll be there to collect you in the morning."

I never gave it another thought and went to bed.

In the morning when I was ready to get a taxi, who do you think was there to collect me? Ahmed with a list of questions! He must have been up all night thinking about all the things he wanted to learn now that he knew I was an international trainer.

Our journey took approximately 20 minutes. Knowing that my time was limited when my contract would finish that week, I used the journey to ask him what his priorities were. His choice was marketing, so I gave him lots of marketing tips that worked for me, and he constantly asked questions so that he fully understood what we had talked about.

Later that evening, he was there again to collect me. Was this man making the most of his positive connections! This time, we spoke about the impact of Positive Words in business and customer service. It is a subject that takes some time, so I could only scratch the surface during our journey. When we arrived at my hotel, he was reluctant to let me go, as he wanted to know what it is about words that makes them positive. To begin with, he couldn't grasp the concept, nor see the impact on customers.

My parting comment was, "To be continued." But this time, we made a firm booking that he would pick me up the following morning. As homework, I asked him to use a couple of the words that we had discussed and to observe the response, if any.

Next morning, he was sitting in Reception, excited because the impact had been strong and instant, which had only whetted his appetite for more. On that morning's journey we covered more words and phrases and the psychology behind them.

When I left his taxi this time, he said, "Have a great day, and it's been a pleasure talking to you. Is that positive enough for you, Liz?"

I said an accompanying smile would make it even better. He laughed and said he would see me at 5.30pm.

His next step in incremental learning was to pull together the First Five Minutes and Positive Words, to enable him to give fantastic customer experiences. What transpired was how he could use this in his life rather than just at work. Then I shared real-life stories how this worked with other people to bring ideas alive for him, so that he could see the many applications. Customer service dealt with, he moved onto the main thing on his mind – marketing!

Ahmed had a list of marketing questions for me on how to build up a database of clients and how to get referrals from satisfied customers. As I'd taught others to do something similar, I was able to tell him the most effective ways to achieve this, which is something I constantly hone. Also, I told him about Bootstrap Marketing Ideas (for the uninitiated: how to pull your business up by the bootstraps by keeping costs low), which totally excited him because then he talked about a business and not just driving a taxi. It truly triggered his entrepreneurial spirit. His excitement was palpable as he could see future possibilities, and I could see that he had really grown in confidence that week.

Ahmed wanted to know how I remain upbeat, because he had noticed that my mood was consistent each day. He reckoned that this must be one of the keys to my success in positively connecting with all sorts of people. For me, this was a huge breakthrough, because I realised that he had truly thought deeply about our twice-daily conversations. He was phenomenal.

His parting words were, "In case I don't see you again, recommend some books I should read to help me make this happen." That was easy.

Do you want to know the best bit? One month later when I was back in Southampton, I happened to meet him as I got out of another taxi. Almost needless to say, he was excited to update me on the growth of this business. He explained that he had set up a database and won himself two large contracts, which provided his bread-and-butter money to enable him to grow his business.

The whole experience had been done step by step, but what a student!

After six journeys of approximately 20 minutes each, Ahmed had completely turned around his business. Just a total of 120 minutes of coaching. Only two hours.

Perhaps you can do that, too!

Connection No. 16
Alain

French Connections

This story is about when you see a stranger looking lost, and how you should always hold out the hand of friendship, as you may never know where this might take you. Sometimes we talk ourselves out of it, but if you can go with your intuition everything will work out fine.

I met Alain from Paris, when I was in Dublin. And here's how we connected.

At the end of my training day, Alain was in Reception at the company I was working with, waiting for a taxi that was never going to arrive, it seemed. Me being me, as usual, I went over to speak to him to see if I could help in any way.

He was so pleased to see me and quickly told me of his plight. I suggested that he share my taxi, as his hotel was in the same vicinity as mine. He accepted immediately and so our connection began…

The desire to communicate was strong.

My schoolgirl French came to the fore, and our word mix-ups were hilarious as we shared stories about our respective families. He explained he was the father of five children while I am the mother of two. During our 90-minute journey, Alain wanted to know what I did for a living that took me away from home. When I explained that I train people to use positive language in business, he was all ears, as he is a Tele-Marketing Manager for a company in Paris. We were off and running. He wanted to find out everything and to understand as much as he could, as this was his particular area of interest, yet he had never heard before about the business application of positive language. We chatted at length, and he requested my business card because he said I spoke with such passion. He asked if I would be willing to work in France if he wished to pursue this further.

I replied, "Why do you think I'm giving you my business card? I've always wanted to work in Paris!"

As it was around Christmastime, we continued talking about families and the festive season. He wanted to take presents back for his wife and children and asked me to recommend shops. I was happy to give him some suggestions, and I arranged for the driver to take him there. However Alain didn't want our conversation to end as he had more he wanted to find out, so he asked if I would accompany him to the shops. I had to decline as I needed to finish packing before flying home, but he hoped we would meet again and said, "Bon Voyage."

Not three weeks but three months later, I received a phone call from the company he worked with, asking me to run a Train-the-Trainer programme, first in London and then in Paris. Naturally, I accepted. Wouldn't you? A month later I met Alain again, this time in Paris. Without question, I had made a strong positive connection because our conversation continued exactly where we had left off in Dublin.

There are no boundaries to positive connections.

Connection No. 17
Christine

A Meeting of Minds

This story is about one of those incidents that happen to everyone who works away from home and has to stay in a hotel on their own. It's all about dining alone and how, by the Power of Positive Connection, you don't have to be on your own any more. When you truly connect with one person, more than likely you will connect with others they know, and this leads to lots of other possibilities.

Christine, or Chris as she asked me to call her, is a trainer that I met in Southampton. It happened like this.

I noticed Chris around the hotel over the weeks I was staying there, but had never seen her in the restaurant at night. However, one evening we found ourselves sitting at separate tables in that special area most hotels seem to reserve for lone businesswomen – you know the one, in the corner near the fire exit? Chris was eating her starter when I passed her table, so I quickly asked how her day had been. She said she was tired, had had enough of her own company, and had decided that evening that she would eat in the hotel restaurant. That was the cue for me to begin our connection.

John, the waiter, also picked up on that cue and suggested I join Chris at her table. A three-way connection. My goodness!

Chris was delighted to have company and we soon found that we had many Me Too's, with similar training experiences. After we had shared a few practical tips, she asked me how I got on with my boss. I replied that I had a fantastic boss who always knew how to motivate me.

She said, "You're so lucky. What's her name?"

I replied, "Liz Hoskin," and we had a fit of the giggles.

Our conversation changed direction at that point and Chris wanted to know all about becoming her own boss. We spoke the same language (no, she wasn't Scottish!) and traded ideas. In the end, Chris shared with me that if she had been younger or we had met some years earlier, she might have decided to set up in business for herself. But she was clear that she did want us to stay in touch as she had a freelance friend and colleague who she felt would benefit from contact with me.

I said I would be happy to speak to her friend, and we exchanged business cards (never leave home without them!). We spent the pudding and coffee time bandying ideas about on how to overcome daily challenges in our line of work… and in our personal lives. It was a stimulating end to an enjoyable meal.

At breakfast the following morning, Chris bounced into the restaurant with a fresh outlook on life and said how much she had enjoyed our time together. And soon after, her friend, Audrey, got in touch with me and I was able to connect her to others.

Always have in mind that when you truly connect with one person, more than likely you will connect with others they know. What better recommendation could you ask for?

Connection No. 18
Fredrick

Find Your Own Style

In this story, you find out that as long as you have enthusiasm and passion for your job, you can be understood by anyone. It's about sharing your enthusiasm and watching how others start to relax into their own style as a direct result.

Fredrick is German, and I met him in England when he was part of an international training team. He is a business trainer for a large company in Germany and was in England to learn new techniques that he would translate into German and use to train his own teams.

I took everyone present through five days of a Train-the-Trainer course, providing plenty of encouragement and feedback. Due to the obvious language challenges, Fredrick's learned style of training was a little stilted, which frustrated him immensely.

On the first day, I concentrated on building a rapport with everyone on the course and gaining their trust, which is second nature to me now. At feedback time at the end of that day, to enable them to make significant progress, I used motivational and formative feedback techniques, rather than the usual pat-kick-pat method. (By way of explanation, pat-kick-pat is known as a feedback sandwich, which covers what was good, what was not so good, and then a summing-up of the whole session. By contrast, motivational feedback is what went well; formative feedback is what can you develop to be even better, and which leaves individuals with a clear development plan.)

The next day proved to be a complete transformation, because Fredrick rocked, and his new-found understanding was infectious to the whole group. He had accepted his feedback because it was clear, and he knew exactly what he had to do to improve. In fact, each day he got even better. On the last day, he asked me to sit down because he wanted to give *me* feedback, which was a rare occurrence. He was a good student and structured his comments in the same motivational and formative style.

He said, "You really know how to connect with your people, Leez. Everyone was given the feedback they needed to make improvements. I love your motivational style and enthusiasm, because it made us feel enthusiastic. How it could get even better is: When are you going to learn German?"

We had certainly connected, and he gave me a huge hug.

He told me, "I have found my style. You helped me find my style, and now I know I am doing the right thing."

What is your style? If you're not sure, just don't try to be someone else. Be true to yourself and you will find it.

Connection No. 19
Peter

A Big Thank You

This is when you have had a strong influence on others, and they want to give you recognition for what you've done for them. The difference in this story is that the recognition can happen in the most unlikely of places.

Peter is an ex-boss of mine from many years ago. He was promoted and had to build a brand-new sales team consisting of a dozen people, including me. This was not perhaps one of my usual connections, but it most definitely was a connection, as you will see. Each week I inspired him with my connection stories, and as he said I had a passion for excellence, he presented me with the book of the same title in appreciation.

Our team became known as the Motivation Squad, because of our enthusiastic style. We met our targets and had fun in the process. We worked hard and we partied hard. Again, because of my tele-marketing expertise, Peter used me as an example to the rest of the team on how to plan weekly sales appointments. In time, we led the field because we met our weekly sales appointment targets and helped each other in the process.

As a result of our success, I featured in a company training video teaching others how to connect with customers, so our fame spread throughout the UK in our very large company. Peter progressed to bigger teams with more responsibility, and he valued my input.

That year, our annual targets were met ahead of time, just before my annual vacation. In passing, Peter asked where I was going on holiday that year and we discovered he was going to the same destination – Majorca – with his wife and child. He asked if my family enjoyed the location, as they were staying nearby. I told him it was absolutely fantastic and that it was where I went most years to recharge my batteries.

We both laughed when Peter commented, "You mean to say I'll come back like you?!"

A few weeks later, I was lying on my sun lounger, blissfully at peace with the world, when I heard a familiar voice saying, "Hi Liz. Bet you didn't expect to see me."

I was startled, and stood up immediately to find out why he was stalking me. He didn't seem the type! It turned out that he wanted to thank me in front of my husband and family, including my brother and his wife, by treating us *all* to a slap-up meal at a restaurant of our choice, with cabs to deposit us safely at our hotel afterwards.

What a thank-you. And what a connection.

His gesture certainly impressed all my family, as they experienced the value of what I do, but things like that seem to happen to me all the time.

I didn't expect anything special from our connection, but if you really connect with people, you never know what will happen.

Connection No. 20
Dawn

Believe in Yourself

This is a special story that, from the outset, I knew was going to be different, as this type of connection doesn't happen every day. The story is about a person I met at a networking event who shared their deepest desires with me and, through following through on those desires, was able to truly believe in themselves. At first, I thought I had failed them, but this was exactly what they needed to happen so they could take charge of their own destiny.

I was attracted to Dawn and her mother, Julie, at one of those not-working networking evenings in Glasgow that I knew I had to attend, even though I had just got out of hospital.

I noticed the two women standing together and thought they looked like sisters. On Dawn's badge it said, 'Just Dawn' and that was my opener...

I said, "Come on, I know you're not Just Dawn. What is it you do, because you look really interesting?" She was beautifully colour-coordinated, and trendy into the bargain.

She told me that she designed children's hats and had a small shop in Castlemilk, near Glasgow.

I asked if she had any hats with her to show and she got out her photograph portfolio which proved what an eye she had for colour and design! As a mother of two, I had never seen anything like them before; they were unique.

When I asked her what she wanted to do with her designs, she told me, "I know I can tell you because I know you won't laugh." That was another sign to me that we had connected.

Her response proved that she was a girl who liked to think big! She said, "I know I can turn around the children's wear department of a national retail store with my designs."

I didn't reply immediately, but looked her straight in the eye before saying, "Take time to answer the next question, because I am totally serious. Are you up for it, because I can help you make it happen?"

Dawn and her mother Julie almost fainted, but this soon turned to excitement. Julie asked how I was going to do that, and I explained that I used to work for the same retail chain she'd mentioned, and still had some contacts there. Even if I didn't have the necessary direct contact, I knew a woman who did.

When Dawn asked what she and I needed to do to progress matters, I asked if she felt confident enough to travel on her own to their London head office. She wasn't, though, and asked if I could be available to go with her. This is not something I would normally do, but I felt she had so much potential that it would be a shame for her to do nothing with her designs.

Julie felt impelled to asked, "What do you get out of this, Liz?'

But I explained that my payback is seeing others fulfil their potential.

Before making any phone calls, I made sure Dawn was serious about her intentions. She was *very* definite. So definite that she wanted me to go with her to London once the appointment was made. And in unison, both mother and daughter offered to pay my travel expenses, which seemed fair to me.

We exchanged details and I said I would make some calls then be in touch in a week or two to let her know the outcome. Within three days I had arranged two appointments in London two weeks hence.

Dawn's reaction? "I can't believe that you, a complete stranger, have done this for me – and so quickly!"

We booked our flights, and I challenged her to spend that next two weeks coming up with more designs for adults, as well as children, because our second appointment was with another well-known retail outlet. We maintained telephone contact during those two weeks and Dawn got her samples, storyboards, and portfolio together before we headed off.

Well organised and with plenty of time to spare, Dawn and I made our way into central London, using the travel time for a final coaching session to make sure that she was quite comfortable and focused on her outcome, which was for either an order or for the company to use her designs.

At our first appointment, we met with the Head Designer, who didn't really connect with Dawn, but he *was* definitely interested in her designs. Dawn decided to terminate the meeting, and outside we agreed that he was more interested in her designs than in her as a person, so she didn't want to work in that environment. Round one for self-belief, because Dawn had made her own decision.

At our second appointment, the Children's Wear Director was "unavailable", so we saw the Retail Director instead, who loved both Dawn and her designs. He kept saying, "As a father, these are some of the best designs I've ever seen, but at the end of the day it's the Children's wear Director who makes the decision about which designs she's interested in." In other words, there was nothing he could do for Dawn.

At that point he asked me what my role was, and I explained to him that I was a Positive Connector. Amazed, he replied, "There must be someone I can connect you with," and offered to connect me with a famous sports personality.

When Dawn and I left, we had a debriefing session and, surprisingly, the outcome of the meeting was that because the Retail Director had been so enthusiastic about her designs, Dawn had decided she would take control of her own future. The whole process had convinced her that her designs were marketable and had given her the confidence to believe in herself and to go for it.

The current situation? Dawn has started to manufacture her own designs.

Self-belief or what?

Footnote: In this experience, the PA to the Chief Executive of the first company was the one who offered to make two connections on my behalf – she set up the appointment with the Head Designer and gave me the contact for the second company. She didn't know me personally, but she had heard about my concept of positive connections and wanted to help me to help Dawn.

Connection No. 21
Joe

Keeping Faith

In this story it would have been easy to be frightened or hold back from getting involved, as it definitely was the most testing positive connection I have ever made.

By working with the person in the story, and not judging, it was amazing to see what started to unravel and how it was all meant to be – or was it?

After a long week in Dublin, this time Joe was my taxi driver on the way to the airport. His first sentence was, "Do you believe in global warming?"

I said, "Yes, I'm sure there's something in it!"

His next question was, "Do you think Princess Diana's death was an accident or a conspiracy?"

To that I replied, "I really don't know."

Third question: "What about September 11, accident or conspiracy?"

Now I knew he was testing my reactions because he had a story to tell.

His final question was: "Do you believe in God?"

I replied, "I believe there is something there, but I don't know if I would call it God."

He said, "Well, I don't believe in God any more because…" and he launched into his story.

Joe had separated from his wife a few months earlier. *Why would God let that happen?* he wondered aloud. I never answered because I knew he just wanted someone to listen to him. He said that twice he had tried to commit suicide, the last time a few weeks earlier when he had rammed his taxi into a wall. I asked what injuries he sustained, and was told, "Just whiplash."

I then asked, "If there is no God, why are you still here?"

That shook him, because suddenly he replied, "No-one said that to me before."

I told him, "I can assure you that if your time was up, you would not be here telling me this story." The response I got was a mixture of tears and laughter, but this was obviously a defining moment for him.

Joe confided his personal situation, and I asked a series of questions for him to try and decide what he was going to do. This conversation took the rest of the journey, but when we arrived at the airport, I simply knew I could not leave it that way. I had to be certain he was going to do something positive and not anything rash, so I was prepared to miss my flight to be sure that he was okay.

By connecting on a human level, just by listening and questioning him, he was able to tell me, "Yes, I have a future. Talking things through with you has helped things fall into place in my mind." I asked for his details (but didn't give him mine, in this instance) to connect him with a support group, then I paid my fare and got out of the taxi.

Joe didn't know how to respond so put out his hand, but I said, "You deserve a hug!"

As an aside, we heard an American tourist nearby say, "Gee, isn't this a real friendly city? Even the taxi drivers give you a hug when they take you to the airport."

Joe and I had a good laugh at that!

Unknown to me, my flight had actually been delayed for half an hour, so my time had been well spent. But was that a coincidence or not?

Two weeks later, when I was back in Dublin and ready to go back to the airport once more, guess who collected me? A much happier Joe, who couldn't wait to tell me his news. He had really made strides in the space of that two weeks: he had reached a better understanding with his wife; got to grips with his financial situation; and found a counsellor to provide him with ongoing support. He wanted to thank me so much because he felt he had turned a corner and had regained his faith in humanity.

Since then, he has started studying part-time at college, as he wants a better future. He told me recently, "I knew the first time I met you that you really cared about people, because there was a bright light round about you, and I knew you had been sent to help me!"

Our connection shows that even when life seems awful and you feel you can't go on, there's always something that happens which enables you to keep faith.

Will you really listen? What will you do to turn another person's life around?

Connection No. 22
Keith and His Mother

Breakthroughs

By helping someone find a way to deal successfully with a situation, the best compliment you can get is when they recommend you to another colleague. This positive connection went a stage further and introduced me to his mother, giving me the chance to connect with the family, and it was one of those moments when you feel blessed just to be asked.

I met Keith in Dublin when I conducted a re-training session incorporating new techniques. Keith struggled because he was from a very traditional call centre background where everything had been scripted, and I could see from his face that the training was not working for him. He was totally frustrated because he couldn't come to grips with the new techniques.

Eventually, I sat him down and asked, "What do you need me to do to make it work for you?" He explained that because he was so used to following a script, he needed some sort of structure to follow.

I knew I could easily help him by suggesting that he colour-coded certain parts of his new call process so that he was comfortable and confident of where he was in his conversation with customers. This took practice, and we even colour-coded the screens he used so that he was completely certain about what he was doing.

As a result, he passed his final assessment with flying colours! And within a couple of weeks, he was meeting targets, really enjoying his job, and sharing what he had learnt with others.

Each time I was delivering training in the company there, he made a point of seeking me out privately to let me know his progress. But one day he had another request, which was a bit unusual. Keith wanted me to help his mother, because he felt I was the only person who could assist her achieve what she wanted to do.

I was absolutely touched that a son wanted to help his mother, so of course I had to do it. I gave Keith my details and told him to get his mother to send me an email.

Carol had just changed careers but seriously lacked confidence. She had landed her dream job as a trainer for unemployed people, but she wanted to find out what kind of further training qualifications were available to add to her development and how she should go about obtaining them. She also wanted to know if I could recommend any books and websites which would support her with her studies. We were email correspondents for a couple of months, and she is now happy in her chosen field, knowing what she now knows.

I also let her know how much Keith believed in her, and how lucky she was to have such a son.

This time, I had connected with two people on two levels, without even knowing it, and it was a pleasure to help them both make their breakthroughs.

Connection No. 23
ABCD Business Connection

This story started off as being very straightforward, and only by following the principles of the Power of Positive Connections – by not doing only what I was asked – did it lead to an evaluation of the future of a business. It let the owners see that communication is key at the core of any good business, and all they had to do was start sharing their passion for the business with each other to get back on track. The ending of this story took the Power of Positive Connection to new heights as something very special happened.

Once, I was asked to be a mystery shopper. To preserve client confidentiality, the people involved shall remain nameless.

The business was in danger of taking a wrong direction and I was asked to find out what wasn't working. By doing the mystery shop, I was able to connect with one of the owners – a lovely guy with the most fantastic customer service skills. In fact, I felt bad that, as part of the exercise, I was not permitted to buy anything!

After mystery shopping, I identified myself and asked if we could go somewhere private so that I could provide him with some feedback. As I was giving him my impressions of him and his shop, a customer entered, so I took the opportunity to observe what went on. After some discussion, the customer announced that she wanted to check if the item was what she wanted and would then come back to make the sale.

When she had left, I asked the business owner, "Do you think she'll come back?"

He answered, "That's the bit I hate about this business. You never know."

So I shared a couple of techniques with him that he could use to ensure he wouldn't lose potential customers in future. Then we really started to connect...

Just by listening, I was able to pick up that he and his business partner had stopped communicating, both thinking they were doing the other's work. Through questioning, we realised that his underlying belief was that his partner was not pulling his weight any more.

I asked what he would like to happen: either to close his business and start afresh, or to continue and keep moaning. And we then evaluated both options. Starting afresh would take him back to square one, which was not where he wanted to be. So he knew they had to sort matters.

I suggested he give me a quick rehearsal of what he was going to say to his partner, and I would give him feedback. This proved illuminating. So much so that by the time we had finished, he knew exactly what he had to say and do. And it was clear that there was no way he was going to give up his passion for his business. I also recommended several books for the future, because he needed to create a sound business philosophy to move forward.

Again, through conversation and connection, everything fell into place.

It took 90 minutes in all, but the last thing I heard was that the partners had sorted out their differences *and* won a national business award.

It's what I call an ABCD – Above and Beyond the Call of Duty. I could have just done a mystery shop and left it there, but I'm sure you know by now, that's just not connection!

Not bad for a mystery shop.

Connection No. 24
My Daughter and Friend

Internet Connection

This story is an emotional connection for all the mothers out there who think they know exactly what their daughters are doing. I thought I did, but this let me see that I had to practise the Power of Positive Connection closer to home. It was a big wake-up call for me and helped me to forge a much closer bond with my daughter. Now we have more than one Positive Connector in our family, isn't life great?

This one didn't start well but – in true positive connection fashion – did have a happy ending, and I include it only by way of a note of caution for all parents.

I have two teenagers. Internet chat rooms? Don't get me started! In this age of pervasive technology, they are a huge danger. But my husband and I always made sure our children were well aware of this.

My preferred style of connection is face-to-face, whereas it is a completely different story when you don't know who you're speaking to.

The first time I realised we had an 'internet connection' was just after Christmas when I was awakened by an early morning call from the mother of my daughter's friend, informing me that my daughter was missing. This totally stunned me, because as far as I was concerned the two girls were enjoying a "sleepover" in our house!

I rushed downstairs to find only one girl – not my daughter – and then the story came out…

It transpired that my daughter had made an internet connection who she had gone to meet five hours earlier. But now she was indeed missing.

I switched into operational mode, taking control. I realised that she had actually been talking to a boy she'd met on the internet – not only through a mother's intuition, but because an unfamiliar number had started to appear on our phone bills.

The next step was to ring that number.

Fortunately, I spoke to both the boy's parents, who reassured me that this was out of character for their teenage son. However, they thought he was surfing in Cornwall with his brother and his brother's friend.

Putting two and two together and not getting four, I tried to piece together the jigsaw and decided to first phone all three boys on their mobile phone numbers. With no success, I called the police, who arrived very quickly because of the internet connection and possible abduction.

As I was filling out a Missing Person's report, reality kicked in – extremely painfully. And it was made even worse when they asked for an up-to-date picture of our daughter, and we began to wonder if we would ever see her alive again.

The next 30 minutes seemed interminable as the police waited for reinforcements. Then, centre stage enters one daughter through our front door, looking sheepish to say the least, with three boys in tow, all looking extremely shaken.

Let's just say that what followed next was a right telling off by both police and parents.

When the police departed, we had time to collect our thoughts. As the boys had travelled all night to see my daughter, I suggested they all go to bed and sleep for a few hours and that we would have a proper talk over lunch.

Listening to and observing all of them, it was evident that they were really nice boys who had decided on the spur of the moment (as young ones do, without thinking of the consequences) to visit Scotland… and my daughter. Believe it or not, she had been extremely sensible and cautious with one of the boys over a period of some months (my phone bill can testify), and knew all about him and had even spoken to his mother. So, it seemed that the situation was very different to what we had first imagined.

The reason she had kept it a secret, she admitted, was because she knew how we felt about internet chat rooms.

I'm glad that we handled everything the way we did, as we had a chance to experience a positive outcome from an internet connection – so much so that before they left later that day, the boys presented me with a box of chocolates and a bouquet of flowers for dealing with it the way we did.

The good news is that my daughter and her new-found friend kept in touch, both families have since met up, and we all made new positive connections from a very shaky start.

The latest update is that the relationship has gone its course and they are no longer connected. However it could have been a whole other story if we had taken a different approach.

Connection No. 25
Frank

Self-Made Man

This is one of those connections that was so meant to be, as everything was against me to start with. However, the universe moved heaven and earth to ensure we connected – like one of those times when your guardian angel helps you just when you need it. I learned a lot on that train journey and was humbled to be in such distinguished company.

Rushing to catch my train home from Aberdeen, I was informed by a guard that I had missed the last train, because services were being cancelled due to heavy rain storms causing flooding on the line. I ran right up the platform and spoke to another guard, who said the train hadn't gone and it was right in front of me. So, if I wanted it, I had better get on right now! He pushed me and my case on, and I took my seat next to a man who looked nothing like the usual "suits" — he was asleep and had kicked his shoes off.

And that's how I met Frank.

I got myself settled and started to read a book, but I couldn't take my eyes off my fellow passenger and willed him to wake up. Within five minutes I got my wish.

As an opener, I asked, "Do you travel by train a lot?"

He replied that he didn't, but he had been for a job interview. When I asked him how it had gone, he said he was confident he had been successful.

I saw he was holding notes in hand, so I asked him what line of business he was in. Frank then told me his story. And he gave me the full picture because, as he said in his own words, he was a self-made man.

Married and divorced due to drink problems, Frank had beautiful daughters he looked after in a really poor area, where there was a complete air of negativity, and no-one was ever expected to do anything.

"You know the kind of place I mean, Liz? Wherever I went, I couldn't escape the desperation of the situation."

One day, he decided he had had enough. He managed to get hold of a gun, and intended to commit suicide and kill his children. But at that moment, he came to his senses, and he realised he was the only one who could get himself out of that mess because no-one else would do it for him.

He went on to tell me the story of his recovery – how he returned to school to get qualifications, moved his family away from that area, and went to university to get a degree in Community Education, while at the same time putting his daughters through college. One daughter won an American sports scholarship.

As he was telling the story of his recovery, I got the picture of someone justifiably proud of his achievements.

Frank then said he had got a job down in England, which had been a success, but because he was away from family and felt lonely, he knew he was in danger of slipping into old habits. One night he realised that he had to get away from that environment or all his hard work would have been in vain. So he returned to Scotland and was offered a job in a community drug education project, but soon realised that he couldn't implement improvements due to management. This frustration led him to get in touch with his former lecturer, who suggested that he should write a book drawing on his own experiences.

And that was why Frank and I just had to connect, because at that time I had just put together the outline for this book.

We continued talking, and he realised that if I could write a book drawing on my experiences, then so could he. We swapped details before parting, and I offered to proofread his book and give him feedback before publication.

What an inspiration. A self-made man, indeed.

Connection No. 26
Train Full of Connections

Tell the Truth

This is a story for all the parents out there who jump to conclusions as to what their children have been up to before asking any questions to help find out the real story. It's about going to the aid of a crying child to help keep them from making an even bigger mistake. We've all been there when it seems easier to tell a little white lie rather than tell the truth, but it helps to look at the consequences and take time to decide the right course of action.

Frank left the train at Dundee, and I continued my journey towards Stirling. When the train stopped at Perth, three giggling teenage girls got on, having just said goodbye to their boyfriends.

Five minutes later the train was hit by lightning, which knocked out the signals on the line and the guard made an announcement that we were going to be severely delayed. Another five minutes later, the guard said that the train would terminate at Stirling, and not Glasgow, due to flooding.

Suddenly, there was a total change in the girls' moods, and I heard crying. Being a mother, I had to respond, so I went over and introduced myself and asked if there was anything I could do to help them.

They told me their story…

They had told their parents they were going shopping in Stirling but, in fact, they had gone to Perth to meet their boyfriends. Oh, young love! But now that the train wouldn't take them back to Glasgow, they were scared of the consequences and knew they would be in deep trouble at home.

I asked what they thought they should do now, but just then one of their mobile phones rang. They recognised the number as being one of their parents and left it to go to voicemail. A minute later, another mobile rang. This time the girl answered, and it was another friend in Glasgow to say that their mothers were looking for them. The caller said she hadn't "grassed" on them; she had lied and said she didn't know where they were.

That's when panic set in.

I took charge by saying, "Look, I can help you because I'm a mother and I know how mothers think. My daughter is about the same age as you are. If my daughter did this, I would prefer to know that she was safe, because not knowing is worse."

They weren't convinced initially, and started scheming more lies to cover up where they were.

I told them, "Right, let me stop you there. Is it not lies that got you into this situation in the first place?"

We then had a discussion about whose parents were the most reasonable, and I even offered to contact their parents to reassure them.

Eventually, the sensible one in the group said, "You know, this lady is right.

We had better tell our parents what's happened because, if not, we're going to be really for it."

I coached them on what to say to their parents then stood back and let them get on with it. Much to my delight, their parents were so relieved to hear from them that they were OK.

Knowing that they weren't going to be in too much trouble, the girls calmed down and I spoke to them again to make sure they were alright. They were all hungry, so I shared out my ever-present travel emergency stock of nibbles while taking the opportunity to let them know my view that it's always best to tell the truth.

They commented that they wanted me as their mother because I could relate to them, but I explained that it was all about connections and listening first before taking action. I added that I didn't know if my daughter would agree with them, and we had a good laugh together.

Telling the truth may seem hard or difficult at times, but it usually works out for the best in the long run.

Connection No. 27
Aine (pronounced Onya)

The Mind's Eye

This is a story which shows that sometimes you meet people who you can connect with at an even deeper level because their interests – or Me Too's – are exactly like yours, or it seems that you are following parallel paths. When you connect with people like this, you spend time sharing what has worked for you and helping each other by making recommendations to assist each other even further. The universe is wonderful at sending you to places to help people develop, and it's always good to be open to new ways of doing things, as this is where you too can develop.

Aine seemed to have a deeper understanding than most when I carried out an induction training in Dublin. During the course, I shared some techniques that I don't normally share about relaxation and visualisation, and she was enthralled.

At the coffee break, she stayed behind to have a chat, wanting to know where I had got that information. I explained that I had just attended a seminar as part of my ongoing education, and that I found the techniques so effective that I wished to share them with everyone. I knew that she and I would have further opportunities to chat over the next couple of days, as we had indeed made a connection.

Next morning, I was in early and Aine was waiting for me, desperate to know all the details of the recent seminar I had attended. I asked why she was so interested, and she told me her story…

Aine wanted to know what made relationships tick. At weekends she was studying about inter-personal relationships and wanted to know more about the techniques I had mentioned because she wanted to experiment. She seemed to have a knowledge of mirroring techniques and visualisation from a book she had read, so I questioned her about these to find out what she knew. She didn't have it with her, but she highly recommended that I read the book she had called *The Mind's Eye* by Ian Robertson. I shared with her the titles of similar books which I thought would assist most – one in particular on visualisation, as this is what fascinated her the most.

After that we shared the Me Too's where our interests and reading overlapped.

Before I left Dublin, she requested information on dates for the seminar I had attended, which I said I would send when I returned home.

As soon as I got to the airport bookstore (which I always do to keep current), on the shelf straight ahead, staring me in the eye, was the book Aine had recommended! I started to read it on the flight home. It was a good recommendation.

Were these all just coincidences? No, they were connections.

Connection No. 28
Jonathan

New Direction

This story happens when you feel in a bit of a rut with your life and, although everything is going along fine, you want something more. By asking questions you can help someone find where their new direction lies and help them to discover it.

Sometimes connections stick around for a while and that's the great thing about the Power of Positive Connection – some of your positive connections can turn into friends and you can be involved with them, if that's what you both want.

I met Jonathan, a South African, as a result of a referral. We had arranged to meet with his business partner in Glasgow at a well-known coffee shop. They both worked as masseurs, while Jonathan was also a personal trainer, and we all clicked immediately.

The two of them were just such good fun and were totally on my wavelength, which is rare on a first meeting. Immediately I knew I had to get them working with me as part of my motivational lunches, where they could provide shoulder and Indian head massages at the end to send everyone away with a unique customer experience.

We had been collaborating for six months when Jonathan came to me one day saying he wanted to find a new direction. He said he wanted to find his passion, although I was convinced that he had already found it. Once we got chatting further, it seemed that his business partner didn't have the same enthusiasm as he did for their work.

I asked him, "Do you really want to go out on your own, because working on your own can be really lonely?"

He said he wanted to be more in control of his own future, and working for himself would provide that. I offered to help him set up his new business – a personal training company – and within four weeks, he was ready to roll. To help him on his way, I connected him with a few of my business connections, one of whom introduced him to a line of products that were complementary to his business, providing him with a second stream of income.

Once he was up and running, we worked together to systematise the structure of his company to ensure success. It's not a job I normally enjoy, but doing it with Jonathan was so inspiring for me as he was so enthusiastic about his new venture.

After a while, Jonathan went on his merry way, and from time to time we re-connect to hear about his latest direction and connections. I love it when a change of direction works out so well for someone, so well.

Connection No. 29
Kate and Tony

Inter-Connections

Have you ever heard of six degrees of separation? Well, this story is about just that, when you have connections that are interconnected for some reason, and everything seems to be pointing towards an even bigger picture. This story is very unique, as it goes to show you that when you have a great idea you should start acting on it, as you never know who might have the same idea.

I mentioned Kate in Connection 5, and she is one of my life-connections. After the Tony Robbins' seminar, we kept in constant touch by email and phone but never managing to meet up because of our hectic schedules, until a six-monthly reunion that Kate regularly organises for a team she is part of – known as the Golden Team 24 from Hawaii. (Tony Robbins has groups of volunteers who help at his many seminars, and they all have numbers, so Team 24 is one of them.) It is so stimulating for me to meet up with such a high-energy group at least twice a year.

On one of my trips south to a television studio in London, Kate invited me to stay with her at her flat in the capital. This time the tables were turned, as Kate coached me through my impending interview. It's just the way we are. We always look at the bigger picture.

Relaxing that evening, Kate asked me, "So what is the bigger picture, Liz? What is your vision?"

I told her the full story of my years of positive connections and where I wanted to take that next, which included the writing and publication of this book – to be followed by others. I also mentioned another simply stunning idea I had about taking connections up another level.

Kate went silent briefly, then said, "Wait a minute, just wait. I have to make a phone call!"

After a few minutes of conversation to brief the person on the other end of the phone, she put me on the line to her friend Tony, an entrepreneur.

What happened next was one of those really spooky moments, because on telling Tony my idea, he said, "You're joking. That's exactly what I've been working on for the last six months. We must meet, and it's got to be tomorrow because I can't wait!" (He knew I was going back home the following evening.)

In the end, our connections expanded, and ultimately five of us met in an hotel foyer in Central London. We shared stories and ideas, and it's truly astounding how thoughts travel and even cross continents.

Three weeks later I was back in London. Dinner that evening was in Tony's home in Surrey, and included Kate and Anthony – one of Tony's friends. What followed has led to amazing inter-connections, with me meeting half-a-dozen like-minded writers, and Kate and Tony visiting a Scottish castle, amongst many other serendipitous happenings and connections.

Incidentally, Kate typed up my first draft of this book to encourage me in true connection style when she came to me for a week's stay.

Connection No. 30
Florian

Never Give Up

This is the final story in the book, and it is about never giving up even when you feel that there is no way out. I'm a great believer that if you keep going it will lead you to a special positive connection to help you continue on your quest. Practise Expectancy and believe in right place right time, and you will be amazed at what you achieve. This story is just the beginning – more will follow, and who knows where this will end?

I met Florian in Paris. Rather, he found me in a restaurant on Saint Michel Boulevard, when he approached our table to offer his printed stories for sale. When he launched into his spiel in rapid French, I quickly stopped him and said, "To save you wasting your time, I'm Scottish and my companion is Australian."

He responded angrily, "I never waste my time!"

Not one to be put off with such a display of annoyance, I got excited because I now knew he could speak English. So I wanted to know where he was from, which turned out to be Montreal, Canada.

My friendly and interested questioning defused the situation and the magic began…

Florian told me he had moved to live in the most romantic city in the world to follow his passion, which was writing. I had no doubt this was his passion because when he spoke about writing, his demeanour and body language lit up the room. He had already been in Paris for four years, but admitted that this had been the worst week of his life because he had sold nothing, and he was on the point of giving up.

Of course, everyone would love to follow his or her passion, but how many do? Yet, here he was sharing with me the realities of following your dream. I am not usually a monetary benefactor, but for the first time ever, I was compelled to give him a small sum of money to enable him to carry on. And my companion felt the same compassion.

Florian was speechless, because no stranger had ever done that before. And already a deeper connection had formed.

My companion said, "Tell him what you really do, Liz!"

At this, I launched into *my* spiel and told him about positive connections and a new project I was working on in the United Kingdom to help people follow their dreams. Florian said he couldn't believe his luck, to which I replied, "Luck has nothing to do with it. Have you ever heard of being in the right place at the right time?"

He replied, "Of course I have, but I never thought it would happen to me."

Florian then wanted to give me and my companion copies of his stories and a CD he had made. I told him to keep them as he would need those to make a living, that this was his livelihood that he was giving away, but he wouldn't take no for an answer. We reached a compromise, and he pointed out a story that he thought could be useful to me for my new project. More questions about the project followed and, because he was so fascinated, I asked if he would be prepared to come across to the UK to take part.

With our growing rapport, he explained about a project he knew about in Paris called "Shakespeare's Library". Shakespeare in Paris? He explained in greater detail to satisfy *my* curiosity and I just knew this was the start of something special. We exchanged details, with me promising to be in touch soon.

I asked to take his photograph – again a first for me. And although he was camera-shy, with a little cajoling he eventually agreed.

Amazingly, when you don't give up, everything falls into place.

And finally...

Some might say I'm lucky and that all these positive connections happened because stuff like that always happens to me. I disagree, as I never see it as luck. For me it is always about the energy you bring into a situation, always suspending judgement, and taking people as you find them. It also involves being open to new opportunities and possibilities, and sharing ideas – a book, advice, or the odd word of wisdom.

My purpose is all about connecting with people to make a difference in their lives and the people who they connect to, by sharing a connection, a book, a tool or technique, or a piece of information which will be part of the Power of Positive Connection.

By sharing some of my stories with you, my hope is that you will be inspired to try the Power of Positive Connection in your own lives – and you definitely won't be disappointed.

As the great inventor Henry Ford once said, "If you think you can, or you think you can't, you're right." Everything you do in life always starts with you. Yes, you! And my whole philosophy is that you get out of life what you put into it.

When I write about things like the First Five Minutes in story four, this comes from research, by observing lots of people and watching how quick a connection can click – sometimes in an instant. However, it can sometimes fade away just as quickly. That's why it's called the First Five Minutes, because by spending five minutes with someone you will know if it's worth staying with your connection or not.

In story five, I talk about Me Too's, and if you get three Me Too's you definitely have a strong foundation to explore things further, Now a word of caution. It doesn't mean that you are long-lost family ☺, it simply means they will understand about where you're coming from and the conversation between you both should flow.

In the world of sales, this is a great indicator if someone will buy from you, too. Sometimes I test these Me Too's when my gut instinct doesn't feel 100% with the situation, and before long you will realise that sometimes people just want to be in your energetic field because it can make them feel good. However, you can easily tell this, as they start to drain your energy very quickly. You have just met a drainer.

Once you identify the drainers in your life, you will realise that you need to limit the amount of time you spend with them. In some extreme cases, you need to let them go from your life altogether, as it's too draining being around them and ends up having a negative effect on you, too.

In story seven, I talk about Blank Sheet™ which is something I have created to help free up people to discover what lights them up. This exercise can even help people to identify the ideal career for them. It's proved to be a worthwhile way to spend half an hour of time on a plane with a stranger, and help them walk off the plane with renewed confidence and vigour for their future and a more fulfilling life.

The Positive Action Plan I mentioned in story nine was written by Napoleon Hill and compiled by Michael J. Ritt and Samuel A. Cypert, and is a Positive Action for every day of the year. It's a good book to refer to when you need a little bit of focus or just to help you remember why you want to be better than yesterday.

I hope you have enjoyed reading my book. I would really appreciate if you can write a review on Amazon or any other review site.

I would love to connect with you so please check out my website, https://positivequalities.co.uk

I spend my life creating new ways of working for businesses and individuals, and this involves me creating tools and techniques to embed the new behaviours and habits. This is something I love so much, and I feel blessed that I have created a life that I don't need to escape from.

To be continued. . .

About the Author

Liz Hoskin is a ray of sunshine that beams positivity and lights up every life she touches.

As founder and Chief Radiator of Positive Qualities Ltd, she helps her clients to transform their business by generating positive energy through supporting and encouraging all members to be their best selves.

Liz is a connector. She sees opportunities everywhere and goes out of her way to help people look beyond what they think is possible. She shares her words of wisdom freely creating impact and generating ripples of kindness across the globe.

Connect with Liz :

liz@positivequalities.co.uk

https://positivequalities.co.uk

Follow on LinkedIn https://www.linkedin.com/in/lizhoskin/

Lightning Source UK Ltd.
Milton Keynes UK
UKHW010634080822
406998UK00002B/526